Preface

I wrote this book to enlighten those who may be inspiring to be graphic designers and are not sure about how to get into the field. This topic is dear to me, as it is my profession and passion. I only wish I would have known more before I started. If I would have had a mentor or known someone in the field, I could have alleviated a lot of hardships. That lack of knowledge made my career option so hard because I literally had to learn and try everything first-hand. I wish for you to not have to go through that. So I took time to write this book (not ChatGPT, but I literally wrote this) to hopefully answer the questions and give real-life insight to those wishing to enter this field. That being said, I would like to acknowledge my wife for believing in me and supporting me through my journey of becoming a graphic designer and author. I would also like to thank my son for being my motivation for teaching others about how to become a graphic designer.

Chapter 1
Let's Get Into It!

What's good? How you doing? I'm your guide on this journey, and hopefully, by the end of it, you'll walk away with a better understanding and some solid skills. So, what's the deal? Well, I'll break it down for you. We're talking about the life of a graphic designer. That's the dream, right? It's definitely my vibe. In fact, it's exactly what I do. What began as a hobby is now my profession.

As I started penning this book, I couldn't help but reminisce about my humble beginnings and how far I've come. I remember that feeling of not knowing, the uncertainty, and self-doubt. You can picture all the bumps and bruises I accumulated, wondering if things could've been smoother with a bit more insight along the way. And I'm not talking about your typical tutorials on tools and software – YouTube's got plenty of that. The term "Graphic Designer" is tossed around so much that the true essence of graphic design often gets lost. Choosing graphic design as a career path becomes this tangled web of perceptions and realities. This book aims to unravel that web.

Let's debunk some myths upfront. Being a graphic designer is way more than what the masses make it out to be. It's not just about designing and being good at it – although that's crucial. There are some behind the scenes moves that many people might not be aware of. I'm talking about the ins and outs of graphic design. We'll be delving into:

What exactly
graphic design is

How to step into the
graphic designer zone

Crafting a
killer resume

Exploring various areas
within graphic design

What makes a
portfolio stand out

Nailing
the interview

We'll explore the typical journey of a graphic designer, the freelance scene, the corporate grind – everything graphic design! Feeling pumped? Ready to dive into the world of graphic design? Let's go!

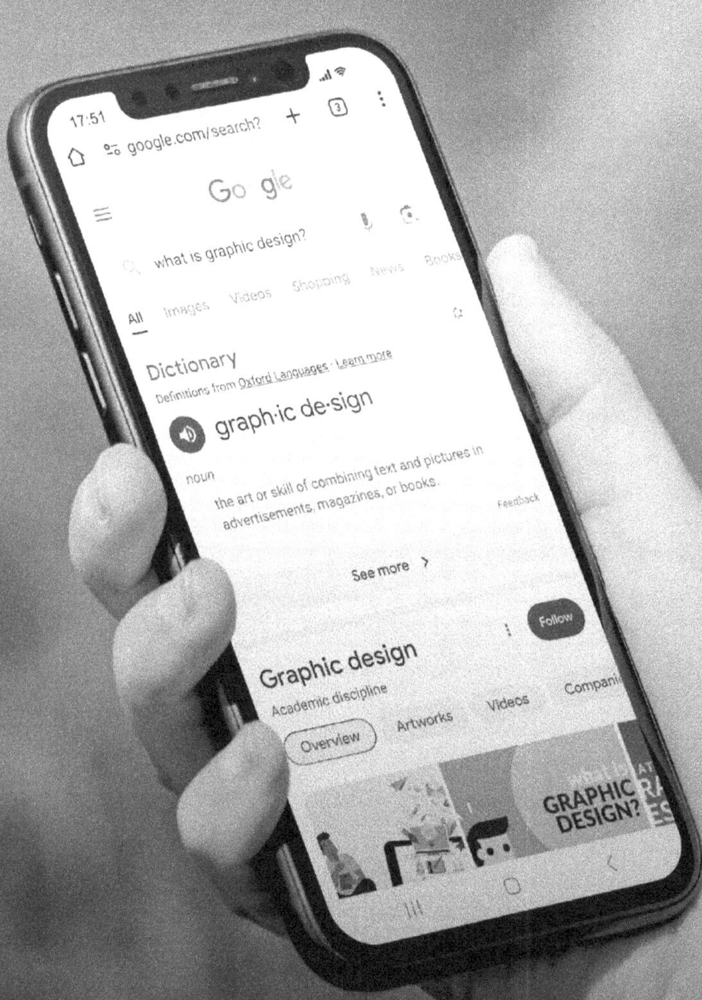

Chapter 2
The Definition

So, what is graphic design exactly? Well, it's not what most people think—it's not just about doing something in Photoshop. Graphic design encompasses a wide range of creative endeavors. For instance, creating logos, like the iconic ones you see on major brands; flyers, for promoting events or products; billboards, the massive ones along highways; posters, for advertising; business cards, your professional introduction; invitations, for special events, and the list goes on, almost infinitely.

Additionally, graphic design extends its reach to unexpected realms, such as lower thirds in video production and even architecture, where it plays a pivotal role in shaping the aesthetics of physical spaces. These examples illustrate the diverse and expansive nature of graphic design, demonstrating that it's more than a single tool or software—it's a multifaceted discipline that permeates various aspects of our visual world. By understanding this breadth, aspiring graphic designers can embark on a journey that goes far beyond the common misconceptions, exploring a dynamic field that intertwines creativity and functionality in numerous captivating ways.

Here are a few visual examples of the different types of graphic designs.

Logo Design

UX UI Design

Flyer Design

Business Card Design

Motion Design

Billboard Design

Presentation Design

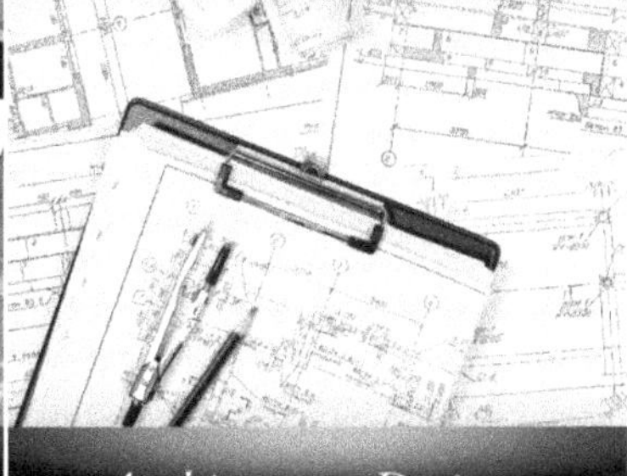

Architecture Design

Contrary to common belief, not all graphic designers are qualified or skilled in every area of the field. Some focus on logos, some on presentations, others on typography. Graphic design embraces a multitude of pathways, extending into video with titles, lower thirds, and logo animation. So, what is graphic design? The Oxford dictionary doesn't quite do this definition justice. Here's my take: Graphic design is the art of visually enhancing and beautifying various mediums.

Now, let's dive into what a graphic designer is. It's anyone who can produce any area of graphic design. Whether you're into magazine/layout design, product design, or any other form, you're a graphic designer. However, we're not all the same. We present ourselves in various forms and don't necessarily have the know-how of each facet of design. Pick the areas you like and stick to those or be a jack of all trades. You should probably dabble in different areas, even if you've found your calling. This increases your understanding and wherewithal for collaborative efforts.

In the end, graphic design is a vast field. Find what you're good at, use your artistic talent, and discover which business or creative field suits your skillset best.

So, that's what graphic design is and what a graphic designer is in a nutshell. Still want to be a graphic designer? I'll bet you do. But don't close the book yet; we still have so much more to discuss!

Chapter 3
How to Learn
Graphic Design

Now that you've gained insight into what graphic design is and the role of graphic designers. If you still aspire to be a graphic designer, the next logical questions are: How do you become a graphic designer, and should you take courses, or should you teach yourself? There are advantages to both, but there are also cons to consider, so let's explore both paths. Before we do, here's a brief story of my journey to "Graphic Design-dom."

From the age of 8, I always enjoyed drawing—cartoon characters, superheroes, and even crafting a comic book. Fast-forward to college, where I pursued web development, earning a bachelor's in computer science, and later, a Master's in I.T (Information Technology). While web development was intriguing, my creative instincts led me to digital design, particularly Photoshop. Balancing website creation and coding, I found myself gravitating more towards aesthetics, often ensuring websites looked visually appealing. Lucky for me, my best friend was a graphic designer. How convenient right? So, any feature or tool I couldn't figure out, I could ask him. My best friend, in addition to YouTube and an affinity to learn, launched my graphic design path. I was getting better and better quickly, and I could physically see it. I was still making websites (I still do), but graphic design had me hooked. I absorbed everything, watching tutorials and practicing designs daily, eventually putting web development on the backburner. To be honest, before gaining experience, I learned everything about graphic design from my friend and YouTube. At that point the only thing I took away from school was some common web design principles that kind of intersected with graphic design. It's also safe to say, I never used my master's degree in any capacity. The interesting part is that I didn't study graphic design formally, but my best friend, offering crucial insights, had a bachelor's in fine art with a concentration in Graphic Design. So, did I vicariously take courses for graphic design?

Now, let's delve into the pros and cons of taking courses for graphic design. Starting with the pros, if you opt for courses, you gain knowledge of rules, theories, and best practices. You receive valuable, critical feedback from teachers and peers on your work and ways to improve. The structured curriculum ensures a step-by-step progression, preventing you from learning "Z" before "A." Additionally, if you thrive on constant instruction, reassurance, or motivation, this route might be suitable for you.

Moving to the cons of taking courses, the primary drawback is cost. Affordability is a concern for those with limited funds, and even those with more financial resources often hesitate to spend. While scholarships and grants are available, not everyone secures them, impacting your pockets. Time is another factor; many courses include historical learning before diving into practical aspects. This means spending months on font history and color theory before using design software. Last but not least, is personality awareness. Your course will not be individualized for you. This means if you really are all about logo design, it doesn't matter.

The course is the course, and that course may just gloss over logo design as it tries to encompass graphic design, leaving you kind of unfulfilled.

Now, let's explore the realm of self-taught learning. The primary advantage is the freedom to learn almost anything about graphic design from the internet—YouTube, Google, and Reddit offer a wealth of information. Beyond the flexibility of content, you have the freedom to learn in a way that suits you. People have different learning styles; some need time to process information, while others require repetition. Personally, I prefer reverse engineering by examining finished products. Additionally, time efficiency is crucial. Unlike traditional classes where the pace is set by the group, self-teaching allows you to learn at your own speed.

However, the cons of being self-taught mirror the pros of taking courses. There's a lack of structure, and you might miss important design fundamentals. Without external motivation, there's no penalty for procrastination or laziness. Moreover, feedback may lack technical advice when the critics are not designers themselves.

Being Self-Taught	Taking Courses
Pros of Being Self-Taught	*Pros of Taking Courses*
Flexible learning pace	Structured curriculum
Personalized approach	Feedback from teachers
Freedom to choose topics	Exposure to theories
No cost (if utilizing free resources)	
Cons of Being Self-Taught	*Cons of Taking Courses*
Lack of formal structure	Cost implications
Limited external feedback	Learning at a fixed pace
Potential information overload	May cover unnecessary topics

In conclusion, a happy medium can be found by combining both approaches. Courses are likely to teach design principles, while self-teaching guides you in specific design processes and tips. For example, a beginner's course might cover font theory, whereas online resources might provide a practical "How-to" video. This combination offers a standard education alongside personalized learning.

So, what's the bottom line? There's no right or wrong—these learning techniques are specific to the individual. My advice is to try both, as each has its pros and cons. You may not discover what suits you best until you've experienced both. However, there's a caveat when it comes to securing a corporate job. When applying, some companies may inquire about your educational background, certificates, or courses. The lack of these credentials could potentially impact your chances. On the flip side, some companies prioritize a great portfolio. If you plan to be an entrepreneur or freelancer, credentials may hold less significance.

Chapter 4
Choosing a
Career Path

By the time you read this, you should be strongly considering yourself as a future graphic designer. But wait…you're not exactly sure about what path you want to take. As I stated earlier, there are so many different types of graphic design, choosing one or a certain field may be difficult without proper context. The fact of the matter is you may not even be aware of the various routes you can take. Without further ado, let's discuss a couple of the most common fields of graphic design.

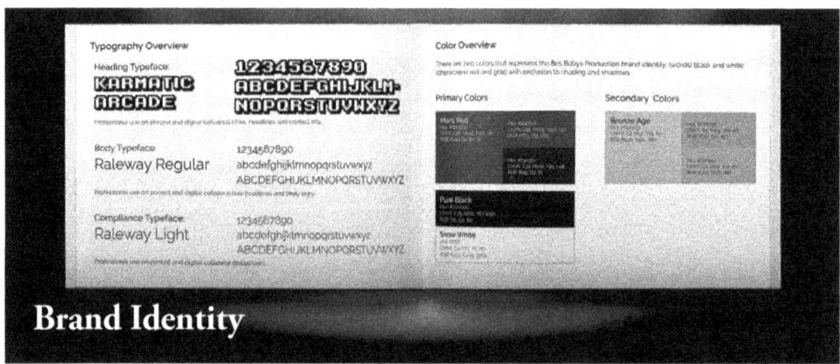

In brand identity, a graphic designer relies heavily on feel and aesthetic. As a brand graphic designer, you're going to make sure that the company that you work for or the company that you create has a specific feel to it. For instance, just say you worked for a company called Angry Man TV. The theme of this television show is a talk show host that is always upset about the topics he's talking about. From that description alone, as a graphic designer, you should kind of understand how this show should be branded. The brand identity designer would pick the suitable colors of this brand. The primary color would probably be a hue of red because red represents anger. When dealing with commercials, flyers, social media posts, product design, websites, everything visual from the logo to the font, it's the identity designer's duty to portray the brand's personality. Graphically the designer would want to stick to angry imagery and bold fonts. These types of graphics convey a consistent tone with the brand, and as a brand identity designer, it would be your job to create or enforce the brand's identity.

This type of graphic design is going to follow the rules of the brand identity graphic designer. It sounds similar but it's not the same. The difference is, this graphic designer makes creative assets under brand identity guidelines and accordingly to the platform in which these designs are being presented. In this career path, the designer can be responsible for an assortment of media such as; flyers, pamphlets, vehicle wraps, postcards, social media posts, infographics, presentations, banners, billboards, signage, etc. All that and much more fall under the marketing and advertising scope. To put it simply this graphic designer will be the driving visual force behind most promo of any given company.

User experience (UX) and User interface (UI) are growing rapidly. In fact, this career path is like graphic design on steroids, as it falls slightly outside the realm of graphic design. Realistically, UX and UI are two separate areas of expertise and design; however, most people and companies lump them together because they heavily intersect with one another. Let's quickly break down these two titles, then it will make more sense as to why they are grouped together so often. UX designers are responsible for…you guessed it, the user experience. This designer is heavily reliant upon data collection via consumer research, target demographics, competitive audits, product equitability, product accessibility, etc. This type of designer only cares that the product (whether it be an app, website, or game) is pleasurable in all aspects for its intended users. This is basically the philosophical aspect of the product. UI designers are on the opposite spectrum. These designers are responsible for making sure the product looks good. They speak to the product's overall aesthetic by means of color patterns, typography, iconography, button design, etc. This is basically the visual aspect of the product. Here's how the

UX and UI intersect. The research of the UX designer dictates how the UI designer proceeds. Here's an example. The product is an app for seniors to take their medicine. The user experience research shows that their target demographic is those aged 55+. The research also shows that people within this age range also wear corrective lenses. Once that data is given to the user interface designer, that designer should be of understanding that the font shouldn't be too small, and the colors shouldn't be distracting. This would be interpreted because if the target audience is likely to have a sight impairment, the design shouldn't make it harder for the user.

This career path heavily leans toward the creation of physical products. This graphic designer is more geared to the knowledge of layout design and design functionality upon different materials and printers. A good example of this type of designer is one who designs magazines. This person is the one who directs how the titles, articles, and paragraphs are arranged on each page. They would indicate this within the realms of how many columns are on the page, how to fit images on the page, the size and type of fonts used, etc. They are also responsible for understanding what type of paper or cardstock the product will be printed upon. This makes the world of difference because stylistically all designs and colors don't work well with all inks, printers, and materials.

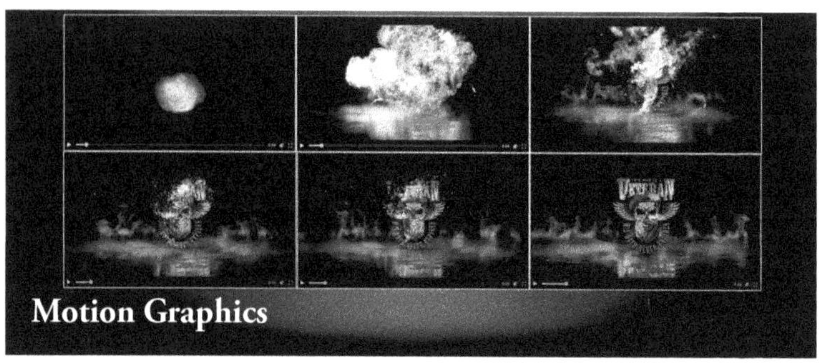

Motion graphic designers are basically graphic designers for video. This graphic designer is equipped with some video editing skills. Their job ranges from lower thirds (the name that pops up at the bottom of the screen when someone is being interviewed) to special effects in movies. A motion graphics designer is one who animates a static graphic design to fit a video format in a variety of ways. Some of the most notable and possibly unnoticed by the average consumer types of motion designs are logo animations. They are so common that they are overlooked. DreamWorks, Lionsgate, and MGM to name a few, are really just static logos, animated. Another instance of motion graphics used in everyday life is titles. These come in the form of intros and outro sequences of movies and TV, all the words seen on the news and the words seen on sports broadcasts.

Now these aren't the only fields of design, there are a multitude of different paths to take and if I go over each area we may never move on. But this is a good starting point, as most other graphic design careers will branch from the aforementioned.

Chapter 5
How Long
Does it Take?

So, you have a firm understanding of what a graphic designer is, how you're going to learn graphic design, and what type of graphic designer career paths are out there. Now you're thinking, "how long is this going to take?" I know, it seems like I'm a mind reader, right? LOL No, I'm not, but these are the same questions I had when I first started. Long story short… there is no answer.

Now here's the short story long. There's no time limit because design is not always logical. In many aspects, art is not science. This means principles can be taught but are not always needed or included, and the exclusion of those principles has no bearing on the success of the design. Furthermore, most graphic designers start from a place of being an artist. They are just people who like to draw, then their talent is nurtured. Take me for instance, as a recap, I grew up drawing names at first. In 2nd grade, I would draw "Bubble Letters" with my classmates' names and charge them 50¢. That was some big money. Then my passion grew into drawing comic book characters, all the while never even knowing graphic design was a thing. As I got older, I wanted to learn how to put my drawings on the computer. My official graphic design journey began. This implies I have been training to be a graphic designer all my life. On the other hand, my elementary school friend never had an art bone in his body. As we got older, he was into party promotion, which he needed flyers. He began creating flyers at the age of 25; that path took him from being a party promoter to getting an associate degree becoming a full-time graphic designer. That's 2 completely different paths into the field and two totally different timelines. So again, there is no specific answer to how long it takes to become a graphic designer.

The real question should be, how long does it take to be a "good" graphic designer? To "master" graphic design? According to the proverbial 10,000 hours rule—often cited for mastering any skill—it would take roughly 417 days of constant practice to become a master at graphic design. This equates to about 1 year, 1 month, and 14 days. However, in real life, no one can dedicate 24 hours a day to learning. On average, individuals may study for about 3 to 4 hours a day. By these standards, it could take the average person around 7 years to master graphic design.

Yet, these estimates don't consider the individual variations in learning speed, innate talent, or external factors like motivation and dedication. Furthermore, graphic design is a continually evolving field, encompassing various art forms, programs, tools, and practices. Arguably, no one truly 'masters' graphic design. The pursuit of being a 'good designer' is subjective and varies based on individual perspectives.

Whether you choose to take courses or learn independently, the key takeaway is that learning in graphic design is a continuous process. As you delve into the world of design, practice and ongoing learning will build confidence, and the appreciation for your work will naturally follow. After all, in the realm of creativity and design, beauty is indeed in the eye of the beholder.

Chapter 6
Corporate vs.
Freelance

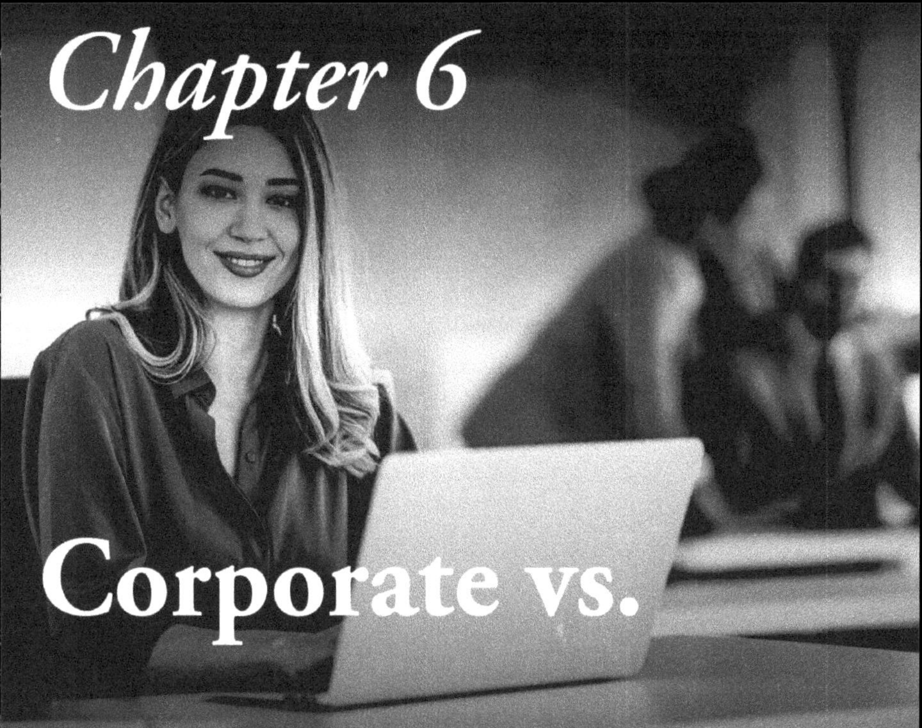

You've decided what type of graphic designer you would like to be, now it's time to get paid. There are two major mediums in which graphic designers generate income: working for a company or freelancing. Some people even do both. Before we go any further, let's delve into them both, and hopefully, you will be able to make a more informed decision on how you would like to proceed in your career. Spoiler alert: "The grass is not greener on the other side"; it doesn't matter what side you pick. There are pros and cons to each.

How about we examine the freelance designer first? A freelance designer is one who works under contract. This contract can range from one project set for a specific duration (normally up to one year). However, the contract is agreed upon, the idea of a freelance designer is not long-term. Contrary to the freelance designer, the agency designer is expected to work for one specific company, forever. Sounds rash, but they hire employees to work for them and for them only, and they generally provide extra incentives to make that more enticing. This leads us right to the first pro and con: stability.

One of the cons of being a freelancer is that there is not a guarantee of income past that single project or the duration of the contract. This scares many people, including myself. Not knowing how you're going to pay your bills two or three months from now is not a comforting feeling. The corporate employee won't have this same issue.
This segues into compensation, one of the cons of the

agency designer is that they have a set amount of income they can generate. In the corporate world, the company offers the employees an hourly wage or yearly salary and possibly some healthcare benefits. That typically is all the employees can earn, barring any bonuses the company may offer. As a freelance designer, there are no limits. Their ability to earn income solely rests upon how much they want to work, how much they want to charge for their services, and how they market themselves to the world. GEM-Hence, there are more millionaire entrepreneurs than salary employees.

That leads us to time. Time is tricky because the actualization of how time is spent varies from person to person. So time is a pro and con to both sides of the argument; here's why. A freelance designer will see time through the lens of not being constricted to a set schedule. Some people are not morning people, so the idea of having to be at work at 8 am is a hardship. Some people only like to work in 2-hour spurts. Some people work faster than others, so they believe it's a waste of time being at work for 8 hours. These are some of the cons of working in a "9 to 5" setting according to a freelance designer. A corporate designer may perceive their time differently. The corporate designer likes the idea of a schedule. This means they know exactly how their day is going to go every day. Yes, there may be a wrench thrown in every now and then, but the overall idea is in place. Beyond scheduling, many freelancers don't factor in the time to find clients. The agency designer will not have that problem. For the most part, once the agency designer leaves the office or logs out for the day, their work is done.

Which brings us to responsibility. "Heavy are the heads that wear the crown." As a freelance designer, you're not only a creative/designer, you're also one who conducts business on all fronts: consulting, project management, copywriting, physical marketing, social media marketing, daily operations management, and finances, to name a few. To a true freelance designer, they won't see this as a con; they would see this as a pro, as they are in total control of everything. The agency designer won't view these responsibilities in the same light. Working in a corporate or agency setting generally means that someone else is handling everything outside of the actual design. Corporate designers, although focused on the project itself, may not have to worry about aspects like client charging rates or finding new clients. They typically handle the creative side while other departments manage various business aspects. Not saying the agency designer doesn't care about anything, but they don't shoulder the same burden as a freelance designer.

All that being said, here's the kicker. I should have prefaced this chapter by saying, most graphic designers will begin their career as freelance designers. This is how you gain your "real-world" experience. It normally goes like this: You do some designs for your friends and family, then they refer you to some of their friends and family. These couple of projects will generally let you know how you feel about working with clients directly and all the pros and cons about freelancing.

FREELANCE

Pros:
Flexibility;
Variety of Projects

Cons:
Unpredictable Income;
Short-Term Contracts

CORPORATE

Pros:
Job Security;
Predictable Income

Cons:
Limited Earning Potential;
Less Flexibility

Pros:
Unlimited Earning
Potential

Cons:
No Salary Guarantee;
No Vacation/Benefit pkg.

Pros:
Stable Income; Benefits
(Healthcare, etc.)

Cons:
Fixed Salary;
Limited Bonuses

Pros:
Flexible Schedule;
Work-Life Balance

Cons:
Irregular Work Hours;
Time Spent for Business

Pros:
Structured Schedule;
Consistent Work Hours

Cons:
Fixed Schedule;
Limited Flexibility

Pros:
Full Control;
Diverse Roles

Cons:
Business Management;
Multitasking

Pros:
Specialized Roles;
Less Responsibility

Cons:
Limited Control;
Focused Responsibilities

The corporate world is kind of consistent across each career path. You do the work and go home (at least until you become upper management). It's less stressful but financially limiting. Is there a right or wrong answer? No, it depends on the person, their goals, and comfortability.

Chapter 7

Making a Portfolio

Now that you're familiar with the graphic design world and have absorbed insights from the first six chapters of this book, it's time to put theory into practice. I hope you picked up some gems that I dropped and you're super ready, right? Finally, after all this talk about becoming a graphic designer, it's time to do some graphic designing. So, you decided what type of graphic designer you're going to be. You chose whether you were going to work freelance or be employed by an agency. Your next step, and this is a very critical step... drumroll, please… making a portfolio.

You may have thought your resume was most important. It is, but it doesn't hold as much weight in the graphic design world as it does in most occupations. In a majority of career paths, you can't physically show people what you can do. For instance, I used to be a security officer. If I were to try to get another security job, I would have to explain what I did on my resume. In that type of role, there was no way for me to show prospective employers what I did. I mean, I guess I could have made a video of me standing in a doorway, pointing people in a certain direction, LOL, but words on a resume would describe that role much better. As graphic designers, our portfolios mean the world. Firstly, all our work is derived from the creation of visually pleasing projects. That in which words won't do our creations justice. I can tell you, "I made the best logo ever! It's a forest green, metallic ball with the words 'Save the Forest' in a serif font inside the ball. There is a hint of neon green highlighting the ball, making it look like it's 3D. There is also a drop shadow on the logo 10px off the y-axis with a Gaussian blur. It's the best logo anyone has created in the world!" Describing one of my projects in this fashion with words and not visibly showing somebody what I am talking about makes me an author, not a graphic designer. This is why making a portfolio is so important. Your portfolio is more than just a display of your work; it's a dynamic tool that showcases not only the final outcomes but also your creative process and critical thinking skills.

The objective of creating a portfolio is to show potential clients and/or employers what you're capable of, as well as your critical thinking process. As a bonus, you can also post this to social media platforms and/or online communities to receive feedback from others (which will help you improve as well). So, what's to this portfolio? What is it composed of? How do you make it?... You have so many questions, but I'm glad you asked. As a beginning designer, the most important task is to start designing. If you've found a niche that's great, but if you haven't, there's no need to be deterred. What you'll want to do is give yourself a deadline and within that deadline, design as many projects as possible. This will not only give you numerous projects to choose from, but the deadline will also make you stop designing and start creating your portfolio.

After you went crazy designing all these beautiful pieces of artwork, the next thing you want to do is have them critiqued. You might be surprised how people view your work. Feedback is a designer's best friend. As artists, we tend to fall in love with our designs because we pour our hearts and souls into them, but we must be open to the opinions of the audience we are presenting to. When it comes to listening to "constructive criticism," don't take it personally, you're not designing for yourself, you're designing for others, so their opinions matter. Also, you have to keep in mind that you aren't perfect, you may design with certain biases that you are not aware of. No, you don't have to do everything that someone suggests, but give it a look. For example, if I made a flyer and showed it to someone, they may say the font is too small. I should take strong consideration of that critique, even though I thought it was perfect. Why? Because I have close to perfect vision and the person critiquing me may not and that small oversight can make or break the success of my design. On the other hand, if I created an image of a comic book fight and the feedback from one person was it should be all supervillains instead of all superheroes. That is a critique that I would not adhere to, because that ultimately means scrapping the whole design based on personal preference and not design flaw. Last but not least, you should try to get some reviews from a person who is in the field. They normally have technical knowledge that the general population doesn't have and couldn't correctly verbalize them if they did notice (i.e., margins, whitespace, shadow, highlights, etc.).

The goal of your portfolio is to gather your best projects and place them in a central viewing location, i.e., a website. Gem – Your Instagram does not count as a portfolio website. Directing someone to your Instagram to see your work is frowned upon. There are various free and paid websites that you may obtain to showcase your work. I prefer the paid version because you can purchase a custom domain name, which physically and professionally looks better when you're presenting it to someone. And when it comes to your portfolio website, investing in a professional domain name matters. A custom domain, like www.clayvisionsdesigns.com, not only looks more professional but also leaves a lasting impression on potential clients or employers. For example, www.clayvisionsdesigns.com looks a lot better than www.clayvisionsdesigns.wixsite.com/clayvisionsdesigns.com. However, if your funds don't allow this step, the look of your domain name can be put on a backburner for now. Your designs being located in a place where they can be accessed is most important. That being said, this does not mean don't use social media to present your designs to the public. As whichever platform you are subscribed to may present freelance or job opportunities.

Another reason and maybe the most important reason that you would like to have a website for your portfolio is that you need context. Here's something I didn't know when I started. Yes, you have all your great final images ready for the world to see, but corporations like to see the process. So, for each project in your portfolio, you should add a description and possibly multiple images. You should add what programs you used; who you did the project for; what problems you encountered; how you solved those problems; how long it took to finish the project; visual steps leading up to the final product, etc. Your portfolio isn't just about showcasing your work; it's about telling the story behind each project. Add detailed context, such as the tools used, challenges faced, and problem-solving strategies. This not only exhibits technical skills but also provides a glimpse into your creative mindset. This really lets Creative Directors view your critical thinking skills. On top of that, with all the mockups and A.I available, it shows that you really did the work and didn't just find some stuff and put it on your portfolio. How would they know the difference without context? Remember, this is what they see before they decide to speak to you, and this is how you speak without being present.

The million-dollar question, and possibly the only question that has no answer is, how many projects do you add to your portfolio site? There's no real answer because this varies from person to person. I consider myself a jack-of-all-trades and I want people to know that. I don't necessarily have a niche and I don't want one. I find joy in creating whatever I want, and you may be the same way. The problem with this line of thought is, depending on who's looking, you're not perceived as a master at anything. It's like being a Swiss army knife.

Yes, you have all the tools, but they are small and inadequate, when I'm really looking for the best screwdriver I can find. I may not even need or want the rest of those tools. This means you must be ultra-selective as to what projects you add to your portfolio website. This goes for those with a niche as well. Now, how many projects should you include in your portfolio?

Quality should always take precedence over quantity. While there's a consensus on having more than 2 and less than 20 projects, remember that too many options can be an overload for viewers. Focus on showcasing your best work, making a lasting impression with each project. How do you know what piece is better than the next? You have to take yourself out of the equation and try to look at it from a perspective different than yours. You have to keep it real with yourself and judge your work against your other works. Also, if you haven't niched down, you only need one project per type of projects. Meaning if I'm a creator of movie posters, comic book characters, calligraphy designs, and product design, I should only pick 1 or 2 of each type of design. This will be hard, and to this day, I have a problem with it. I'm always creating something new I feel is really nice and I want people to see it, but we have to understand when we give people too many options, they can easily become overwhelmed. I compare it to Netflix or Amazon Prime, it's so many movies, I can't figure out what to watch. I wind up looking through the movies for 2 hours and then saying, "it's nothing to watch". Also, if a hiring manager is looking at portfolios all day and yours is close to the 100th portfolio they've seen today, it's likely that they won't get past the 10th project you have on your portfolio. It will be just your luck; your 11th project was your best project on your portfolio.

Reflecting on my own journey, creating a portfolio has been a personal yet transformative experience. I've crafted numerous portfolios throughout my career, each iteration prompted by various factors. Initially, it was a response to the enhancement of my skillset. As my personal goals evolved, transitioning from aspiring corporate designer to entrepreneur, my portfolio adapted accordingly. Influences from other designers, shifts in my graphic design focus field, continuous skill enhancements – the process keeps progressing. Recently, I found myself creating yet another portfolio; thus, this remains an ever-evolving aspect of my professional journey.

Chapter 8
The Resume

It's been a long journey, and now you should feel ready
and confident that someone will hire you. At this point,
you should probably feel like Adobe should be sending
you an email asking you to work for them. Whoa there,
cowboy… LOL. That's not exactly how that works, but
if it does work for you like that, my hat's off to you.
However, for the majority of us, there are still a couple of
things left to do that will assist in landing that dream job
or just a job, period.

Now that you have your portfolio in order, the first
step to getting employed is making a resume. Most
people are aware that you need a resume when applying
for employment, but what they don't know is what
information to put on their resume and how it should
visually look. How is your resume being received by
hiring managers? What is too much? What is too little?
How far should you go back in your history? All these
questions are legit questions, and for most, they cause
a great amount of concern, which is warranted. So, let's
shine some light on the subject. But first, here are a
couple of visual examples.

DISTRACTING RESUMES

Resume Don'ts 1:
- Too many graphics
- Not enough information
- Doesn't portray why they're a good fit for employment

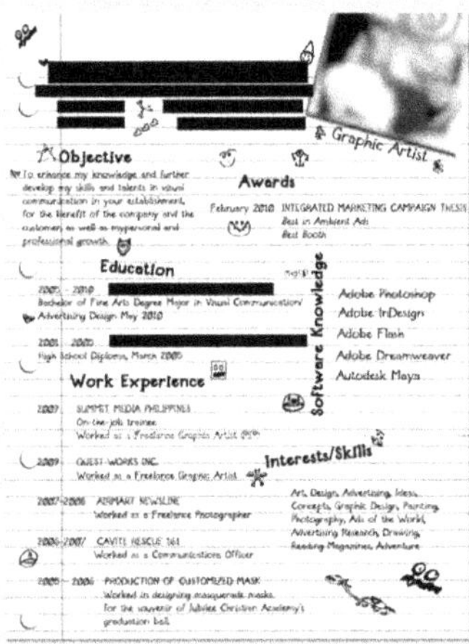

Resume Don'ts 2:
- Very erratic
- Hard to read
- Sloppy design (margins, spacing, in-line text)

Appealing Resumes

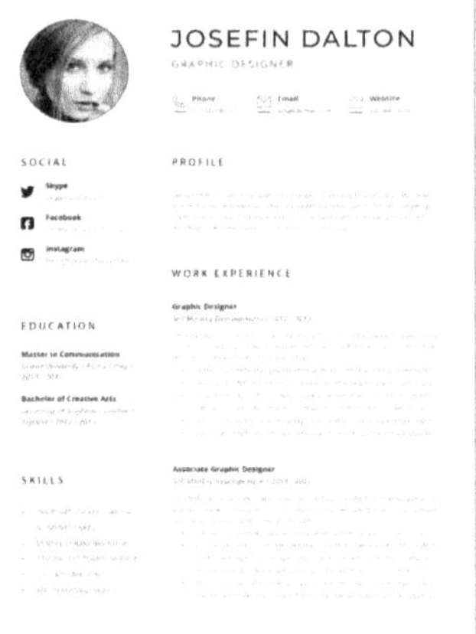

Resume Dos 1:
- Formal
- Concise formatting
- Easy to read

Resume Dos 2:
- Clean Design
- Concise formatting
- Easy to read

*most employers are not fond of infographics

Now that we got visuals out of the way, let's talk content. The first thing you'll want to add to the resume is your header. This includes your name, title, and a link to your portfolio website. Your title will be whatever career path you've chosen to tackle and possibly a secondary title.

For instance, as a motion designer, my header would prominently display my name (IamV), followed by my title in a slightly smaller font (Motion Designer/ Animator), and a link to my portfolio website (www. clayvisionsdesigns.com) in a smaller font. This header will indicate to the hiring manager who you are, what position you want to be employed for, and how to find your work if they are interested.

After you've added your main header, you may want to add an "About Me" section. The About Me section is controversial; some people believe it's not needed; some people believe it should be added. In my experience, when there are conflicting ideologies, I believe a safe space is somewhere in between. That said, a concise 2 to 3-sentence biography (around 50 words) serves as a compelling introduction. This is basically an introduction stating what you're about and what you're capable of. This is what you want people to know about you before they know anything else. Think of it as a 2-sentence tagline, like MasterCard – "There are some things money can't buy. For everything else, there's MasterCard," but a little longer.

Next, we will add the work history. However, you name this section (Work History, Previous Employers, History, etc.), should be separated into a different section of your resume, with those words in bold so there's a clear separation. This part of the resume gets tricky, mainly because some people have an extensive history, and some people have a limited or non-existent history. No matter your specific case, the fundamental structure will remain consistent. First thing to note, if possible, do not add anything that does not pertain to the type of job you're applying for. This applies across the board unless it is your only work history, or your history only has 1 job in the field you're applying for. For example, I used to drive a forklift. No context of that job crosses over to graphic design; it's completely irrelevant. The only way I would add that job is if I don't have any graphic design experience (no freelance or anything), and then it provides context that I understand job responsibility. Next, we want to add the name of the company, the dates of which you worked at said companies (month and year), and your title at that company. These titles will spearhead each job individually and in chronological order from most recent to past. Below that sub-header of the job title, the job description is inserted. GEM – You want to keep each job description to a minimum of 3 and a maximum of 5 bullet points. You want to keep your bullet points at a low number because you want to highlight the important aspects of your job you performed and not have someone who is scan reading your resume overlook them in a sea of words. Also, this is where a majority of your keywords will reside.

Keywords are very important to a resume because many of the job boards (that we will talk about later) are assisted by an ATS (Automated Tracking System). This ATS filters resumes by scanning keywords in your resume against words used in the job posting, which then decides whether or not your resume reaches the hiring manager.

Next is the skills section, sectioned off just like your About and Work History sections. This is where you place more keywords. It includes the software that you use, the different computer languages you are fluent in, and other soft skills like communication and leadership. The skills section is crucial for the hiring manager to assess your proficiency in using the same programs they use and gain insights into additional aspects of the job where you excel.

After you've added your skills, you should include your Education. I like to look at this portion of the resume as icing on the cake, or brownie points. It shows discipline, formal knowledge (which is interpreted as technical capability) and pending what school you went to or courses you took, the value of knowledge received. This includes the name of the school, degree obtained, years attended, and G.P.A. (Grade Point Average). Now for those like myself, who have been out of school for 5 years or more, the dates and G.P.A are not mandatory. You should add any corresponding courses or certificates you have attained relevant to the career path in this section as well, and just like your formal schooling, they should have corporation names, dates, and certificate titles.

Lastly, in a tiny section, your contact information needs to be added. Email address, and phone number are the only things in this section. If the hiring manager or recruiter needs to contact you for any reason, they will have reference here. GEM – Make a professional, up-to-date email address. This matters: if your email address is something like mizzhottie19@yahoo.com or igetmoney2@gmail.com, you're likely to get passed on. The yahoo account makes it seem as if you're not current, and those handles make it look like you may not be suitable for a professional setting.

Wow… I know, that was a lot, but we're not done. From what I have assessed, the visual aspect is mainly a problem for designers because we tend to want everything to look good and stand out. From what I've gathered from a multitude of hiring managers and agencies, we're not wrong. Hiring managers tend to get bored from looking constantly at all text resumes. Yes, the resume is there for them to read, but who doesn't like a graphic novel? It just changes the monotony of looking at black text on white paper. With that in mind, your resume is not a flyer either; it can be over-designed and then become a turn-off. So, we have to find a happy medium. Light graphic design is preferred on resumes. If you're going to use designs on a resume, you should stick to 3 colors maximum. The design should not overshadow the text by any means. Use the colors as accents (like bullet points, section separators, borders, and elements of that nature). If you choose to use actual graphics, keep them clean and sleek, with the usage of small iconography and light pattern design. It can be visualized as a less graphic-heavy infographic. For those of you who have these types of graphic design resumes already, know that the loading-bar style skills portion is seen as obnoxious. You know, where you have the title Photoshop then a loading bar next to it or below it that reads 79% or the bar is ¾ full. It just shows a lack of confidence; there are a handful of people that are 100% in Photoshop, the hiring manager or recruiter just want to know if you're proficient and with it being on your resume, it's self-explanatory.

Should you put your picture on your resume? Maybe… This might be the one question in which the answer I don't know. The verdict is so back and forth on this subject that it really depends on who you ask. In one view, one would say if the hiring manager liked the way you look, you might have a better opportunity at getting the job. On the other hand, they may not like the way you look. I know that's beauty bias or lookism which is wrong, but humans are… human. Many of our actions are based upon how we feel when we see things. I don't think that it can be avoided. My argument is, what happens when I get an interview and they see me and don't like how I look? The rebuttal is, they've come too far to turn back, and you may be able to win them over with words. But then I'm stuck with, do I even want to work for people like that? Point I'm trying to make is that there's no right or wrong. If you feel your face may give you the edge, go for it. If you feel your face may cause a problem, get your confidence up. You look how you look, so be proud of it. Beauty is in the eye of the beholder, and there is no one who is ugly to everybody; keep that in mind.

Apologies for the beauty rant… LOL I just had a lot to share, and I want everyone reading this to feel confident. Let's avoid judgment! Moving on… Let's talk about the length of the resume. In my opinion, it's good practice to keep your resume to one page. However, sometimes this is just not possible. If my employment history includes roles like 3 years at Google as a Creative Director, 1 year at Amazon as a Lead Designer, 3 years at Disney as an Art Director, 2 years at Apple as a Brand Identity Designer, and 1 year at Adobe as a Visual Designer, it's essential to include all these experiences on my resume. But if I wake up, and I'm just me, LOL, my resume can do without that random contract job I had for 2 weeks and that freelance job I did for 1 day. In this case, I can cut my resume size down significantly. I can also add those experiences to a single job title of Independent Contractor and have my freelance responsibilities and duties fall under that umbrella. It's normal practice to not go further back than 10 years unless that employment is extremely relevant or important to your history. Some examples of this would be if you worked for a company for over 10 years that leads into current time or, without that company, there's a huge gap in time of employment. We also must keep in mind the reader. Do you really expect someone to read through a 3- or 4-page resume with integrity when they have hundreds or thousands of other resumes to assess? It's not realistic, so we want to hit them fast and hard. All that said, we should try to keep our resumes to 1 page, or 2 pages max.

After you've inserted everything you want in your resume, it's time to format it or prepare it for export. Personally, I like to create my resume in InDesign; you might use Illustrator or Word, it really doesn't matter. What matters is how it is exported. GEM – You should export your resume in two file formats, Microsoft Word and .PDF. The reason for the two formats is simple, and I wish someone would have told me about this. When you export your resume as a Word Doc., everyone who receives your resume may not have the same version as you. This leaves room for your resume to break. Many companies do not use Word; therefore, they may have an old version, or you may have an older version. All versions of Word don't crossover effectively. This means when you send a beautifully formatted one-page resume, there is a chance that your resume once opened in a different version looks terrible. It could wind up destroying the tables, columns, and margins making it look like you have no idea what you're doing. This leads the hiring manager asking, "Why would someone send me an eighteen-page resume?" Where does that resume wind up? Trash! This is exactly why you want to have a .pdf version. These formats don't break, if they are opened, they will look as intended. On the flip side, sometimes .pdf's can be too big in file size, so you would want to have a word version just in case. Having both formats will assure that you're ready for anything.

Chapter 9
How to Get
the Job

Okay, now it's finally time for the meat and potatoes. You know what career path you want to take. You're confident in your portfolio website. Your resume is on point. Let's get paid to do what we love! Let's get a job! WARNING: THIS STEP IS NOT FOR THE FAINT OF HEART, AS IT MAY REQUIRE TIME AND DEDICATION.

Let's start here. Where do you want to work? I mean, like if you could work for any company in the world, what company would that be? Well in our job search we will start there and work our way down. The saying goes, 'If you shoot for the moon, you may miss and land on a cloud.' That may not be it, but it's something like that. LOL The point is, aim high and see what happens. Don't aim low and place a ceiling on yourself. You never know, your dream company could be looking for a beginner, because beginners are easier to mold. Your dream company could love your work because they see your potential when others don't. You let them decide. My mother used to always say, 'If you don't try, you already failed.'

Before we start applying for these jobs, let's create a spreadsheet. This can be done in Microsoft Word with the use of a table or in Microsoft Excel. This spreadsheet will help you keep track of the jobs you're applying for. I like to make columns for: Company Applied To; The Position I Applied For; Date I Applied; Salary (if listed); and The Response from the Company. There are a couple of reason why you want to have a spreadsheet. The first reason is because it is looked at as unprofessional to apply for the same job more than once within a six-month span. The employer sees this as you just applying and not paying attention to who you're applying to. They like to feel special, so if you apply to their company more than once, they feel like you don't really want to work at their company, you just want a job. The second reason to create a spreadsheet is for the exact reason those "employers who want to be special" are talking about. You are going to be applying for so many jobs that you may not remember. So, every time you apply for a job, you enter it in your spreadsheet. My best friend was in a similar circumstance where a company called him in for an interview. He thought they were calling him in to be a 3D artist, but they were calling him for the graphic design position he applied for. If he would have created a spreadsheet, he would have known. Instead, he went to the interview unprepared. In light of situations like that, just consider this spreadsheet as good record-keeping and something that can prevent you from feeling like an idiot in the future. All-in-all, the spreadsheet is not only for tracking job applications but also for avoiding duplicate applications within a short time frame. This helps maintain professionalism and prevents annoyance to employers.

Here's an example of one of my old Google Sheets spreadsheets. You can use my template or create your own.

	Company	Position/Type	Pay (highest)	Found On/ Applied On	Date	Response	Reached out/ Person Contacted
1							
2	Lyda Fire	Senior Graphic Designer/Remote		LinkedIn / Lyda Fire			Audrey Anderson
3	Medterra	Senior Graphic Designer/Remote		LinkedIn			
4	Jerry	Senior Product Designer/Remote		LinkedIn / Jerry		NO	
5	CapTech	Senior UI/Visual Designer/Remote		LinkedIn			
6	Aspen Dental Management, Inc. (ADMI)	Senior Graphic Designer/Art Director/Hybrid		LinkedIn			
7	Notable	Sr Product Designer/Hybrid		LinkedIn/Notable			
8	Braintrust	Senior Designer/Remote		LinkedIn			
9	Athletic Greens	Product Designer		LinkedIn/Athletic Greens		NO	
10	CyberCoders	UX Designer		Indeed			Allison Taylor
11	LogicGate	Product Designer/Remote		Indeed		NO	
12	Leo Burnett	UI / Digital Designer/Hybrid					Jen Johnson
13	John Deere	UX Designer		Indeed/John Deere			
14	Stericycle Inc	Visual Designer		Indeed			
15	Purple Drive Technologies	UI/UX Designer				NO	
16	Braflon	UX/UI Designer/Remote		Indeed			
17	Perkins&Will	UI Designer		Indeed			
18	Walmart	Designer Lead - Content Design Lead		Indeed/Walmart			
19	Fetch Rewards	UI Designer/Hybrid		Indeed/Fetch		NO	
20	PerkSpot	Senior Digital Designer		Indeed		NO	
21	Deloitte	Senior Designer-Deloitte's Green Dot Agency		Indeed/Deloitte			
22	ZipRecruiter	Senior Product Designer/Remote		ZipRecruiter			
23	Pathfinders Advertising	UI/UX Designer/Remote		ZipRecruiter		INTERVIEW	
24	Addison Group	UI/UX Designer/Hybrid		ZipRecruiter/LinkedIn		NO	
25	HireMilitary	UI UX Designer/Hybrid		ZipRecruiter/HireMilitary		INTERVIEW	
26	Reward Gateway	Product Designer		ZipRecruiter/LinkedIn			
27	UX Hires	Product UX Designer/Hybrid		ZipRecruiter		NO	
28	1871 Member Companies	Manifest - UI/Graphic Designer		ZipRecruiter			
29	Zeno Group	Senior Designer/Hybrid	$112k	ZipRecruiter			
30	Razorfish	Senior Designer		ZipRecruiter			
31	Vizient, Inc.	UX Designer		ZipRecruiter		NO	

Okay, here it is application time. Starting with the companies you think you want to work for and some research. The research serves two-fold. It will allow you to see if you fit your future company's culture and if their culture fits you. For example, many people hold religion in high regard, if you were a devout Christian, you may not want to work in an unapologetically Muslim environment and vice versa. Or if you're a member of PETA you may not want to work with a company whose primary client is Kentucky Fried Chicken. Here's a real story, I didn't do my research on one company that I got invited to an interview with. Long story short, I wore a suit to the interview and they literally told me, "You're a little over-dressed." So, safe to say I didn't get that job, they didn't believe I fit their culture. Now you get my drift. After you do your research, you'll want to go to the website of every company you want to work for, find their career link and see if they're hiring for your position. If they aren't or you can't find a link, don't hesitate to send their Human Resource Department or their company an email. Sidenote: If you don't have a LinkedIn account, make one.

About 98% of employers use LinkedIn to evaluate potential employees. A LinkedIn profile also allows you to:
* Help Hiring Managers and Recruiters Find You;
* Strengthen Your Resume/Application;
* Manage Your Professional Contacts, Past and Present;
* Network;
* and Build Your Professional Brand.

If you can't figure out how to contact the company from their website, someone in their company definitely has a LinkedIn account. Contact someone there.

Beyond directly contacting a company or corporation, let's attack some job boards. This is where you'll find the random companies. Well, they're not random but there are so many smaller unfranchised companies that you may have never heard of it seems like randomly named businesses. My personal favorites for corporate jobs (in no specific order) are LinkedIn, ZipRecruiter and Indeed. You don't have to use all three, or any of these for that matter but they're my go-to's. These websites provide thousands of design jobs, and they have search filters such as: job radius, date posted, desired salary, employment level and much more. Another reason I like these sites is because they have apps, which means you can get real time notifications to new jobs and responses to your applied jobs. Besides that, these websites also offer quick apply sometime. Once you've created an account, they store your information and resume. With quick apply, you apply to the job with one button. I don't know if you've ever filled out a job application, but that can be a painstakingly long process. Quick apply will become one of your best friends after a few long applications.

What you will find after looking through the job posting on these boards is, a lot of these jobs very similar in terms of requirements and job description, but they have different titles. The reason for these discrepancies is what I said in the beginning, a lot of people don't know how to properly label the graphic design field. That in addition that there is so much overlap in the fields, there is really not a specific name. What do you call a person who makes social media graphics, and is proficient in web coding? That's not a real field, so they may just call it "Visual Designer". With this knowledge, no matter what the position is labeled, once you read the job requirements and feel confident in your ability to perform, apply. Here's where extra steps are involved. If you feel really strong about a certain job, like "Oohh, I would love to work here!", then you would want to revise your resume accordingly. What I mean is, seek keywords and change your title on your resume to whatever the title is on that job. Earlier I mentioned the ATS (Automated Tracking System), this is where that is in full effect. The more keywords in your resume versus the keywords in the job descriptions raises your proficiency level to the ATS. It also peaks the interest of the hiring manager. Once you change your title on your resume, they don't feel like they're looking at a Graphic Designer's resume who could be a Visual Designer, they feel like they're looking at a perfect candidate. Yes, it's playing tricks on the system, but like I said if you really want the job, you have to appear as perfect as possible, because there's hundreds of other applicants. On top of that, the title doesn't necessarily hold any weight in comparison to the job requirements. So, don't feel bad about it. Just think about all the people who missed out when they changed the title Janitor to Custodial Engineer, it's the same job just a different title.

This strategy also works on the form of job description. For example, I wouldn't generally have typography on my resume, just because I feel it's incorporated in the term "graphic design". However, if typography is labeled in a position that I'm interested in, I need to find a way to add that specific word in my resume. If the responsibility is listed in the job requirement, then they want a candidate that can perform that task. If it's not on your resume, they'll assume you can't do it.

Another course of action you could take, would be reaching out to hiring agencies. A hiring agency is generally a third-party company hired to find employees for another company. From my personal experience, I like this option of finding employment the least. With that being said, that's my opinion, and they do work well for some people. The hiring agency serves as the "middleman", they recruit and screen potential employees. They take your resume, give you a soft interview and place your information in their database. Then if they are hired by a company to find an employee with your skillset or title presently or in the future, they refer you. From there you get an interview with the main company. Sounds sweet right? My main problem with the hiring agencies is they are paid per employee they get hired. This incentivizes them to submit as many applications as possible. So, when they call you and schedule you an interview, they get your hopes up high. I went to so many interviews with hiring agencies, it wound up feeling like a waste of time. Little do you know, you're interviewing to be a part of their database, not to get hired. That sucks! On the other hand, I have been employed through a hiring agency once before, for a contract position. So it can work, I just don't like getting my spirits high and then realizing the whole process may be for nothing.

See you youngsters nowadays, have it easy. Back in my day, it was gloomy; we had no internet, no cars, I had to walk 12 miles to each interview… No, I'm kidding, but finding a job can be hard, disappointing, and disheartening for some. This is especially true for those without mentorship and a shoulder to lean on. For many of us, this will be a long journey. My journey into getting into the field, fresh out of school, took almost 2 years. If I'm going to be honest with you and myself, I wasn't trying hard the first year. I was applying for about 10 jobs a month, barely scratching the surface. Then when I really started trying hard. I amassed 10 pages of the spreadsheet over that next year. That was over 350 job applications and about 20 interviews. It got rough for me, and I wanted to quit. I began to doubt myself and my skill level. Even though I had plenty of freelance clients previously that heaped my praise, my confidence began to wane. Luckily for me, my wife was in my corner supporting me and reassuring me that I was good enough, that was my shoulder to lean on. Contrarily, one of my co-workers landed the job we were working at, while still taking courses for graphic design and to be honest, no disrespect, I was much better than him. Was it my interviewing skills? Was it my portfolio? Was it my resume? Was it my appearance? Why was it so hard for me and not my co-worker? I'm not sure. Maybe it just wasn't my time. Whatever the case was, I was dedicated to becoming a graphic designer. And I did just that, with some dedication and hard work. Keep in mind, if your path isn't smooth sailing, doesn't mean you quit. It means you go harder, make necessary adjustments, and persevere. My favorite saying is, "You miss 100% of the shots you don't take." That just means take your shot, because you'll miss the opportunity if you don't go for it as well.

Chapter 10
The Interview

Congratulations! You've landed an interview. Now, let's dive into how to prepare for it. You've completed your portfolio; your resume is nice, and you've been applying for jobs. Everything is going as planned but it's about to get real. You have received an email and a company is interested in you and would like to schedule an interview. No matter how many interviews I have had and trust me I've had hundreds, I still get the same feeling every time I get this email. Excitement, followed by panic. You get excited because obviously you want the job, but then you begin to panic because you want to do a good job in the interview. What if they don't like me? What if I can't do the job? What if they ask me something I don't know the answer to? What if…? If that's how you're feeling, you have to slow down, remove all the self-doubt and trust in yourself. This is where opportunity meets preparation. Let's talk about preparation:

It is very important that you research the company to the best of your ability. The first step in preparing for an interview is knowing exactly what the company is, what position it is that you've been selected for and what the requirements of that job are. Within this research is gaining knowledge of the company products/services, recent news about the company and the company history (many of these will appear on the company's website homepage, if not, there's always Google). This may seem like you're "doing too much" but the information you gain through this research will help you to have talking points during the interview, while making you seem you're genuinely interested in their company. Sometimes the hiring manager will provide that information, sometimes they won't, but if you followed my steps about keeping a spreadsheet of all your job applications, this won't matter. Interviews are tricky, as the interviewing styles from company to company vary. However, talking is always a part of the interview. The hiring manager wants to get to know you better. They want to get a feel of confidence and listening skills. They also like to know if you're really interested in their company or are they just a job to you. With that being said, the first step in preparing for an interview is studying the company. Once you receive that call or email to schedule an interview, you should immediately go to study the company. This will help you generate questions that you can ask the interviewer. The reason why this is so important is because you may have applied for a job thinking more about the actual job than the company. For example, you could easily apply to be a graphic designer for Burger King, every company needs a graphic designer, so you applied. You know Burger King is a big company this would be a good look for you. However, you don't eat fast food, so you have no idea what's on their menu or what their website or app looks like. If you were to receive an interview with Burger King and did no research that interview will probably go terribly as you couldn't relate to the hiring manager what you would bring to the table (no pun intended) or speak on specific products that you could re-imagine. For reasons such as this, research is mandatory. It helps you engage during the interview process on another level. Companies want to know you're interested in a career with them, not just a job and a title.

That leads us to the next step of the research process. The next thing to pay close attention to are the job requirements. I know sometimes these job requirements are sort of ridiculous. They be like "we're looking for a graphic designer that can fly airplanes, create marvel quality movies and do taxes." LOL Looking at the job requirements and knowing what type of company it is will kind of tell you what they are really looking for. Many times, the "real job requirements" are in the description not the bullet points. Your goal is to try to be proficient as possible in as many areas as possible. One of the reasons why you want to focus on your proficiency is because some interviews consist of tests, either in person or after the "meet-and-greet" portion of the interview. From experience, I can tell you the in-person tests are pressure. They are timed and they generally just give you a prompt not telling you what they're really looking for. For example, you may have an interview and they say, "Can you make a flyer with Adobe Illustrator?" Of course, you're going to say, "sure". They're going to give you some details about what they want on the flyer and give you 30 minutes to create said flyer. That is why you should study your craft and your design strategies versus the job requirements, so you can possibly have faster processes. If in fact you find yourself in a position where you don't know exactly what to do, complete the portion that you can first. Take a mental note on the part that gave you a "problem" and speak to that when you submit your test. GEM – The interview tests aren't looking for great artistic value, they're looking for working knowledge and the ability to complete a task. So don't try do make the best design of your life, make sure you finish. Other tests are "take-home" yes that allows you more time, but many times these tests are more difficult. Even with the take-home tests a rule of thumb is to submit them as fast as you can.

Okay now that we've done our research, we are ready to walk into this interview with our confidence way up. But wait…there's more preparation to be done. Let's talk about confidence vs. self-awareness: Some people are natural conversationalist, some people are introverts, some people are low energy, some people are high-energy, some people lack confidence, some people are arrogant. At this point, you have to recognize what type of person you are in conversations with strangers. Self-awareness will help you work on your weak points for an interview. Your confidence in yourself, will show through body language. It will also show in how you speak, not necessarily what you say. You want to make sure your good at keeping eye contact. You want to make sure you're speaking "matter-of-a-factly" as opposed to sounding as if your statements are questions. You want to make sure you have good posture. You want to expound on your answers to questions, no one word answers.

UNCONFIDENT INTERVIEWEE

- **Posture**: slumped down in seat, looks bothered (*bad posture*)
- **Facial Expression**: blank facial expression (*interpreted as uncertain or worried*)
- **Eye Contact**: side-eye (*interpreted as untrustworthy*)

CONFIDENT INTERVIEWEE

- **Posture**: sitting up in seat, leaning forward, looks engaged (*good posture*)
- **Facial Expression**: smiling (*interpreted as inviting, or happy to be there*)
- **Eye Contact**: looking straight into the interviewers eye (*interpreted as confident*)

Keep the conversation going. You want to make sure you have positive energy. You want to be smiling, enunciating, and avoiding saying filler words like "um" and "you know what I'm saying" as much as possible. When speaking with someone who pays attention, those filler words come off as you being unprepared or unsure. You want to ask questions because after all you are interviewing their company as well. On the other end of the spectrum, you don't want to over talk either. If you have any socially awkward feelings about yourself, now is the time to address them. You can practice with someone your close to, after that maybe practice with someone your kind of close to which can make it challenging. There are also websites that offer virtual practice interviewing experiences. Some of these interviews can be intimidating, sometimes there's two or three people interviewing you at once. Sometimes the interviewers can be intimidating so the goal with this preparation is to be the best version of yourself. If you are uncomfortable in interviews, prepare to be uncomfortable. It's okay, just think about it this way. You're one step closer to achieving your goal.

That's it, you did it. Knocked it out the park! You've got one last step. That's sending a thank you email. This email should be sent 24-48 hours after the interview. The thank you email helps two-fold; it shows appreciation, and it brings your name back up to the hiring manager. It makes them have to think about you, again. Remember, 9 times out of 10 you're not the only prospect, so any edge helps.

Hopefully I have answered all the questions you had about graphic design. If I haven't don't hesitate to contact me at https://clayvisionsdesigns.com or any social media platforms @clayvisionsdesigns. I do this for you, and nothing will please me more than helping you with your success. Thank you for reading this and don't forget to check out my some of my content and subscribe to @ clayvisionsdesigns on YouTube or TikTok! Thank you again for your support! Also, stay tuned, as I am in the process of writing the next book. I don't have a name for it yet, but it pertains to starting your own business as a graphic designer.